MAR 2015

CARING FOR HORSES

Creative Education • Creative Paperbacks

Valerie Bodden

Published by Creative Education and Creative Paperbacks
P.O. Box 227, Mankato, Minnesota 56002
Creative Education and Creative Paperbacks are imprints
of The Creative Company
www.thecreativecompany.us

Design and production by Chelsey Luther
Art direction by Christine Vanderbeek
Printed in the United States of America

Photographs by Dreamstime (Simon Evans, Ewilkerson,
Isselee, Sawitri Khromkrathok, Sergey Lavrentev, Anastasia
Shapochkina, Stanko07), Getty Images (Bob Langrish),
Shutterstock (Cattallina, Perry Correll, kislovas, Charles
Knowles, Andrzej Kubik, Nattika, Inga Nielsen), SuperStock
(age fotostock, imagebroker.net, Juice Images, Juniors)

Library of Congress Cataloging-in-Publication Data
Bodden, Valerie.
Caring for horses / Valerie Bodden.
p. cm. — (Horsing around)
Summary: A narrative guide to caring for horses, from where
to house the animals, how to groom them, how much to
exercise and feed them, and what to wear and expect as you
perform daily tasks.
Includes bibliographical references and index.
ISBN 978-1-60818-470-5 (hardcover)
ISBN 978-0-89812-833-8 (pbk)
1. Horses—Feeding and feeds—Juvenile literature. 2.
Horses—Grooming—Juvenile literature. 3. Stables—Juvenile
literature. I. Title.

SF285.5.B63 2013
636.1'083—dc23   2012049911

HC 9 8 7 6 5 4
PBK 9 8 7 6 5 4 3 2

TABLE OF CONTENTS

BRUSHING UP

YOU pat your horse's neck. Then you start to **groom** its coat. You use one brush after another. When you are done, the coat shines!

Grooming cleans the horse's coat of mud and sweat.

4

STARTING OUT

THERE are many steps to taking care of a horse. First, you need to go up to your horse with **confidence**. Touch it lightly on the neck. You might even give your horse a treat!

Horses like to eat pieces of carrots as treats.

STABLE HOME

MAKE sure your horse has a good home. Some horses stay in a **pasture**. They need a shelter for when the weather is bad. Other horses live in a building called a stable. Some owners pay to keep their horses at a **boarding stable**.

This stable has room for 45 horses to live in it.

MUCKING OUT

YOUR horse's home needs to be kept clean. You need to **muck out** its stall every day. Use a shovel and a pitchfork to scoop up droppings and dirty bedding. Put everything dirty in a wheelbarrow. Then sweep out the stall. Put down fresh straw or wood shavings.

Mucking out is messy and smelly but has to be done.

DAILY RIDE

MAKE sure your horse gets exercise every day. **Turn out** your horse at least once a day. Or take it for a ride.

Horses like to stretch their legs and run in a pasture.

FEEDING TIME

HORSES need to be fed many times every day. They can **graze** in a pasture. Or they can eat hay. Some horses need horse feed, too. Make sure to give your horse fresh water.

Horses grab food with front teeth called incisors.

REGULAR GROOMING

GROOM your horse every day. Brush your horse with a **currycomb**, a **dandy brush**, and a **body brush**. These tools help get rid of dirt. Use a wet sponge to clean your horse's face and under its tail. Use a hoof pick to dig stones out of its feet.

You can talk to your horse while you groom it.

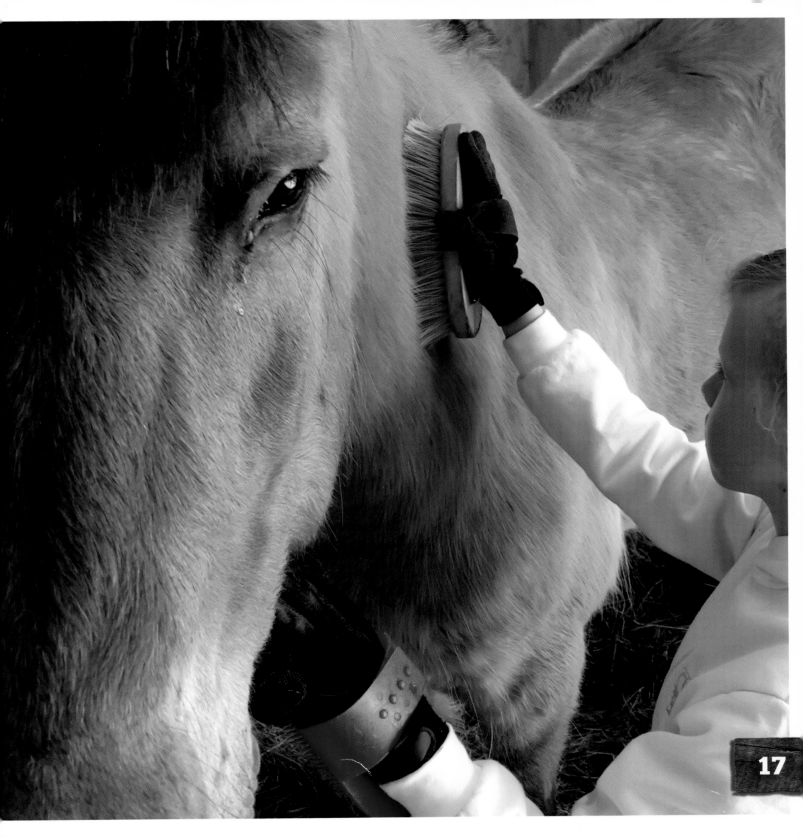

WHAT TO WEAR

WEAR boots with hard toes when you are caring for your horse. Wear old clothes for mucking out your horse's stall. It can be a dirty job!

Rubber boots are good to wear for mucking out.

THE END OF THE DAY

WHEN you are done working with your horse for the day, put your tools away. Taking good care of your horse keeps it healthy. And it helps you and your horse become better friends!

It is easier to find tools when they are neatly stored.

HORSE DICTIONARY

boarding stable: a stable where owners can pay to keep their horses if they do not have a stable or pasture of their own

body brush: a brush with short bristles that help get dirt out of a horse's coat

confidence: feeling brave and sure, not scared

currycomb: a comb made out of plastic or rubber, for getting mud and loose hairs off a horse's coat

dandy brush: a wooden brush with long bristles for getting dirt off a horse's coat

graze: to feed on grass in a field or pasture

groom: to clean an animal's fur or coat

muck out: to clean out a barn or other place where animals live

pasture: land covered with grass for animals to eat

turn out: to let loose in a pasture

READ MORE

De la Bédoyère, Camilla. *Horses and Ponies*. Irvine, Calif.: QEB, 2010.

Pipe, Jim. *Horses*. North Mankato, Minn.: Stargazer Books, 2007.

Ransford, Sandy. *Pony Care*. Irvine, Calif.: QEB, 2011.

WEBSITES

Enchanted Learning: Horse Printout
http://www.enchantedlearning.com/subjects/mammals/horse/Horsecoloring.shtml
Learn more about the parts of a horse, and print a picture of a horse to color.

How to Groom a Horse
http://www.youtube.com/watch?v=MYITqmE_pf8&feature=related
Watch a video about grooming horses.

Every effort has been made to ensure that these sites are suitable for children, that they have educational value, and that they contain no inappropriate material. However, because of the nature of the Internet, it is impossible to guarantee that these sites will remain active indefinitely or that their contents will not be altered.